Kites

Kites

Poems

JONATHAN CHAVES

RESOURCE *Publications* • Eugene, Oregon

KITES
Poems

Copyright © 2025 Jonathan Chaves. All rights reserved. Except for brief quotations in critical publications or reviews, no part of this book may be reproduced in any manner without prior written permission from the publisher. Write: Permissions, Wipf and Stock Publishers, 199 W. 8th Ave., Suite 3, Eugene, OR 97401.

Resource Publications
An Imprint of Wipf and Stock Publishers
199 W. 8th Ave., Suite 3
Eugene, OR 97401

www.wipfandstock.com

PAPERBACK ISBN: 979-8-3852-4455-3
HARDCOVER ISBN: 979-8-3852-4456-0
EBOOK ISBN: 979-8-3852-4457-7

03/27/25

Some of these poems have appeared in *Chronicles: A Magazine of American Culture, and Academic Questions*.

Children With Kites by Feng Zikai (Chinese; 1878–1975)
    Inscribed to the right top-to-bottom are two lines of verse by the poet, Huang Ding (1828–1880) from his poem, "Village Living:"
        "The children, let out of school, come home early
        And rush to catch the easterly wind to let loose their kites."

To Catharine Savage Brosman
with admiration and gratitude

CONTENTS

Kites | 1
Anna's Languages | 2
Troubadour Verses for Anna | 5
50th | 7
A Ballade of Vestigial Hope | 9
Ballade of an Inquisition | 11
Ars Anti-Poetica | 13
A New Proof | 16
An unusual dialogue for which the poet cannot take credit as the concept was devised by a 12th century Chinese forerunner | 17
Antiphony | 19
While Listening to Static Blues | 21
At Salon de Zen | 25
Cormorants | 26
Ballade of Summer Sadness | 28
Malmesbury | 30
Bea, Abbey, Garden | 31
A Print by Brueghel | 33
Face to Face | 34
Où est la vaillance d'antan? | 35
Father | 37
For Sophie Lam | 38
France or China in Prospect Park | 39
Grey Potomac | 40
In Memoriam Steve Berg | 42

In memoriam Tom Bertonneau | 43
Lament for Prince Philip | 44
In the Waiting Room | 45
Man Before a Painting | 49
In Western Turkey | 50
Just One Leaf | 51
The Paradox | 53
Mundaka Upanishad | 54
Ode to an Artichoke | 55
Orientation for Students Going to China | 56
"Our goal should be a planet with fewer humans" | 59
Through Green Mist | 61
Image of an Image | 62
Sonnet for a Wronged Man | 63
Sonnet to Alexandria | 64
Stars and Soul | 65
To Steve Addiss | 66
In Memoriam Stephen Addiss | 68
Cooling Rain: Time tricked? | 70
Daughter in Search of.... | 72
Tanuki | 73
The Absconding of Joel | 75
The History of Four Blips | 77
The Only Antidote | 78
The Physicist and the Bee—A Dialogue | 81
Third Party Harassment | 82
Thoughts on a Photo of Kai | 84
Thoughts on the "Cucumber-Shaped" Object from Outer Space | 85
Unmasking | 87

The Dean Addresses the Faculty | 88

Welcome to the Institute | 90

Ye Earlie Historie of Ye Trepane | 93

Chanson de la nuit | 95

Ordination | 97

Christmas | 99

Presanctified | 100

Pentecost | 101

KITES

These are the kites
they slice the blue air
like knives
their lines
swell with the wind
as they bow to each other
and rise again.
They strive with the birds
to see who can fly higher
but sometimes fall
clutched by trees like dragons.
The children play with them
and know they are alive
when they flutter
in the wind
etching their lines of memory
against the clear sky.

ANNA'S LANGUAGES

When first I saw you,
first heard you speak,
body language
pulled me towards you
mind language
intertwined with long-dead
(so I thought)
places in my mind,
love language
for your children
won my heart, also dormant
but here revived. English
not your native tongue
you handled as a master
in discourse, poetry;
Greek heard
in conversations
sisterly built
Parthenons
within my soul.
On ship's deck,
in Greek sunlight
washed clean
Ritsos you read to me
Greek, then spontaneous
translation into English
true as poetry.

How many languages
had you? And more
you added, Spanish
in conversation
with cleaning ladies,
and with Neruda's poems
flowed next, and French
flows now, a wave
of beauty you've ridden
up above the waters
to a higher then the highest wave,
in just days,
writing of villages in Greece
bringing life to them,
tears to readers' eyes.
Food language just last night
spoke love, compassion,
unplanned, spontaneous
as if snatched at once
through the veil
between the ordinary
and the beyond, back
from there to here
on blue-green plates
jade-like, earth-like...
Music flows, language
of *agape* from the soul,
but your voice
channels heart as well
and joins them
at that central point

where God dwells
in us and above
allowing you to hear
the mourning of the ages
on islands or in Mani
or along *farangis*
of the north and
bring this too
through that invisible veil
here, language
of singing tears.
How many languages
has Anna? I ask myself,
The answer lies
not in numbers—
As the apostles
at Pentecost
spoke all languages
and these all were one,
hers are all in one. . .
Yours are all in you
and of you and speaking you
to me, to others:
All of them are heard
by God, by cleaning ladies,
by birds and squirrels
whose languages too
you have fed back to them.

TROUBADOUR VERSES FOR ANNA

ANNA! How can I
at all convey
what I would say?

You are the air
breathed by the trees
a gentle breeze

Yet are the whirlwind
roaring through the wood
cleansing bad for good,

You are cicadas' chant
Beneath bird-song
all summer long,

The snow-flakes' whisper
soft and low
from falling snow

Here in Languedoc
you are pure wine
a smile divine,

In blue chiffon
the châtelaine
of the Domain

Your hand in mine
you soothe the night
you are the day.

50ᵀᴴ

for Anna

"In these things lies a deep truth—
I would express it, but have lost the words."
   —*T'ao Ch'ien (365–427)*
      Translation by Jonathan Chaves

I know this poem must fail!
T'ao transcended the great paradox
And used words to convey what is beyond words.
Then you and I? Together in marriage 50 years?
And still as I look into your grey-green eyes
I see the glimmer of love,
I see the ocean of friendship,
I see us on the sand or pebbles,
In the water of impossible blue,
On pathways shaded by innumerable trees....
I see mirrored there
My own soul
As it is mirrored nowhere else
But in God's mind.

But none of this suffices
For what I wish to say to you,
I aspire towards what I cannot reach
In words, or maybe at all....

Could it be that a Sun will rise
That never sets,
And we will be together
In that transfigured land
And finally see all in all,
Be all in all?
And will we know
What 50 years have formed us for?

And will we write together
A poem that will not fail?

At this moment
May my eyes at least
Convey it all to you,
Without words,
In simplicity,
From my heart.

A BALLADE OF VESTIGIAL HOPE

Our students now are taught to hate the past,
    To search for "equity," not for what's true.
Civilization—will it thrive and last?
    Or will our "educators" all undo?
    Do we live in a temple or a zoo?
I search for some great rock to hope upon,
    But cannot find a single one—can you?
Yet tourists flock to see the Parthenon.

We're underpinned by what is great and vast,
    By what is sacred, ever found anew
As we build that which gives the ship a mast,
    So there's been hope to pass horizon's blue.
    Meanwhile of vicious sharks there lurks a slew—
If they're unchecked we all will soon be gone
    (Environmentalists are not a few),
Yet tourists flock to see the Parthenon.

Barbarism? Love for sharks? No zest
    For Beauty, Truth and Goodness? Only new
Artificial Thinking? What a pest!
    But we need real thinking now in lieu
    Of what is merely programmatic stew.
Thus how long until the aeschaton?
    It is the final reason that we grew!
So tourists flock to see the Parthenon.

L'envoi

    Pericles! You gave the world a view
Magnificent at dusk, sublime at dawn!
    Barbarians desire to "cancel" you,
Yet tourists flock to see the Parthenon.

BALLADE OF AN INQUISITION

The message unexpected—from the blue—
    Said, "We are writing to communicate
That students in your classes say that you
    Made them feel *uncomfortable* of late;
    Believe us, we do not say this in hate,
But '*Bias Incidents*' wave flags of red!"
    I asked, "Would you the details relate?"
"*We will not tell you what they say you said.*"

Inquisitors of quite a modern hue,
    These apparatchiks asked to set a date
For us to meet, upon which, "We'll review
    The things you said or did to sour their fate."
    A second time, with poison on my plate,
I asked politely if they'd ease my dread
    By writing me post haste their case to state:
"*We will not tell you what they say you said.*"

In Spain the Inquisition took the view
    That heretics at least before the gate
Of Hell closed on them would receive a due
    Account of errors made, without long wait;
    Fodder for the GULAG, torture-bait,
Had their list of no-no's to them read
    Before they found themselves packed in a crate;
"*But we'll not tell you what they say you said.*"

L'envoi
O Chief Inquisitor! If I could sue
Yourself would slowly tortured be 'til dead.
But I am powerless, because, *parbleu!*
You will not tell me what they say I said.

ARS ANTI-POETICA

I make my own "antiquity,"
    wipe out our gang of "heroes!"
Some say it's like "cutting jade,"
    and others, "cutting bronze:"
Let them theorize away,
    blathering "East Qi" nonsense.
When true inspiration comes to me,
    the sea can't be dammed up:
Mysteriously probing the 10,000 things,
    I roam the Vast Expanse!

    —Wu Changshuo (1844–1927)
       on the art of seal carving
           Translation by Jonathan Chaves

Do not set a theory and then write;
Do not set a theory, then translate.
Cart before the horse, you won't arrive
At Mt. Parnassus, whether dead or live.
If you live today, an extra weight
Threatens to expedite your fate:
Our "heroes" like to call it merely "Theory;"
Of their blather you must be quite leery.

We use words, but "Meaning-feeling lie
Beyond the words:" with Mei Yaochen descry
This paradox profound, or with Gilson[1]
See thought incarnate in the word—*Pardon*,
Know they are two but thought appears to us
Only in the word, hence all the fuss
By Linguists of the groves, who grow so blistery
Confronted by the action here of Mystery.

Do you reject Creativity?
Or Imagination? Blessedly
The writer *and* translator have them both,
And on the truth of this I take my oath.
"The Eternal Body of Man," quoth William Blake,
"Is The Imagination," and in the wake
Of this grand claim, "that is God himself."
Take your dusty Blake down from the shelf.

And when it comes to literary translation,
We confront a further transmigration
From Word to Spirit, back to Word at last,
That is, they're two-in-one. To hold them fast,
Unclasp the fist that desperately now grasps
Your precious "Theory," take in mighty gasps
Of purer air. That's better. Now relax.
Write with a quill, not with a battle-axe.

---

1. Etienne Gilson (1884–1978), *Linguistique et philosophie* ("Linguistics and Philosophy: An Essay on the Philosophical Constants of Language," 1969; posthumously translated, 1988).

Do you demand I *prove* all this is true?
I cannot do it. What I can, I do
And find it works, results in equal poems
Related to originals in old tomes
Which reading, time and space are both transcended,
A realm is entered where both minds are blended,
And no experiment can be devised
To measure what is deeply realized.

God gave Adam gift of naming: "Name
The beasts!" And gives us all the very same.
But only few can reach the peak supreme
Of what will perdure, make others dream.
This view is ancient, rather timeless, time
Obliterated by Eternal rhyme.
Put aside Marxoid "historicism,"
And view the world through the poetic prism.

A NEW PROOF

Yes, translation's possible, proud critic!
The beauty carries, most of all, the soul;
Whatever's lost is made up by a whole
That resonates—it is not parasitic.

Today again the mystery of the woods,
The streams, the wheat conveys the heart of Christ,
What He meant when He sent the *Heilige Geist*
To urge the wealthy to sell all their goods,

And find new riches in the misty sky,
The humble carving of a peasant's God,
These treasures answering the question, "Why?"

—The kingfisher's fire, peas set in a pod:
Sharon Fish Mooney gives us Jules Breton,
En anglais—la beauté, la vérité, le bon.

AN UNUSUAL DIALOGUE FOR WHICH THE POET CANNOT TAKE CREDIT AS THE CONCEPT WAS DEVISED BY A 12TH CENTURY CHINESE FORERUNNER

Hsin Ch'i-chi just drank too much,
    or so he thought.
He told his wine-cup, "Get thee hence!
    The health I've sought

Demands you leave! Please tell me not
    of old Liu Ling,
heroic drinker that he was,
    and do not sing

His *Ode to Wine*—a masterpiece
    and yet the one
Work he ever wrote, because
    when it was done

His subject matter was exhausted—
    nor praise him for
his servant who would follow him
    from door to door

And down country lanes beneath
    a heavy shovel—
To dig his grave when dead of booze
    right there! To grovel

Before such heroes is beneath me!
    No, I say
That I am done with drink, so sworn
    this very day!

And yet I fear I might give in
    if you insist
On hanging round. Begone! And now!
    You won't be missed."

"Ah poet, do you fear me so?
    Such fear
proclaims thy weakness over wine
    and maybe beer

(although it's yet to be invented,
    but one time
I bend the rules of history as
    I need the rhyme.)

But yes, I feel for you, and so
    I will obey;
Since you thus dismiss me I
    will go away

But leave you with a promise: Should you
    change your mind
And summon me again, I'll come:
    I'm always kind."

ANTIPHONY

for Jannica Sophia Porcu

Male and Female, Left and Right,
Moist and Dry, and Dark and Light.
Yin and *Yang* from ancient times
Have been China's polar chimes
Ringing cosmic Harmony,
While on earth, there's You and Me,
Couples who embody all
Before and also past the Fall.

Microcosm of the whole,
Church deploys the echoing soul,
Participating in God's mind,
And singing of all things we find
Around us as we pass along
The road of pilgrimage in song.
Music thus above and here
Best transcends all doubt or fear,
Two make one in harmony
Between two choirs' antiphony.
Down from Heaven come the singers,
And their every note long lingers;
Right: Subdeacon with his crew,
Left: *Sophia*, always new,
Always fresh, angelic voice,
Angelic manner, not her choice

But by God's finger on her brow,
Chosen vessel, glowing bow
Asail towards harbor's warm embrace,
And blessed unveiling of God's face.

WHILE LISTENING TO STATIC BLUES

for Graeme Wright Denniss
(To be read slowly in dragged rhythm)

And what rough beast, its hour come round at last
Slouches towards Bethlehem to be born?

—Yeats

i variation three, heard first

We dance
So slowly
With the
Beast all vague
Move so
Languidly
Like ocean wave
Creeping
In staggered largo
Up the strand

We don't smile
But passion's there
Microtonal melisma
Dyes the air
Dark blue
While vapors

Swaying the vast void
Stare dully, cruelly
With eyes
All unaware

ii whole piece

Blues stand still
Or barely crawl
Then slip, slide
Into the Slough
Of Despond
Help has not arrived
Nor Hope; Bunyan's
Pilgrim has missed
His road; life
Calls not
The horn of despair
Wails
Calls not
To the hunt
The Hound
Of Heaven
Pursues not
That
of the Baskervilles
Glitters intermittently
Across blank moors
Teeth, fangs
Would be relief
To denizens of this soul-swamp

Yet denizens there are none
Beside... him
He who wrote
This lament
But sings it not
"Recollected in
Tranquility?"
No. Lived. Now.

Yet redemption
Far off flickers
From piano keys
In darkened
Kafka Café

Mozart, Brahms
Lennox Berkeley
Awaken, disturbed
The cosmos
Repopulated
By kindred souls
They hear the whispered
Wail of grief
And move with infinite slowness
Towards horn, piano,
Violin, extend pale hands
Take hold....
False eternity
Exposed as Time retarded
Pray with them
Pray with me

For final yielding
To Timelessness
To Light.

AT SALON DE ZEN

A hand to trim my hair
Descended like an angel
    Through the air.

And I just sitting there,
Aging, aging, wondered,
    Is it fair?

Eros and Agape:
Must we choose between them
    To be happy?

But the cut was snappy...
Soon behind the wheel
    Feeling sappy.

CORMORANTS

Azure waters splashing black rock—
perched there impossibly
black birds—
"Cormorants!" you said
watching for fish.

All—the spray,
the colors,
waterside rocks,
wafted fragrances our way. . . .
bringing anxious thoughts
back to the past

or the past forward
to now.

Jiang Kui
Chinese poet
12th century
writing of lotus, red,
withering,
and viewing them
with him, a woman
like a swallow
now far away
impossible to touch
or see. . .

we share the perfume
of sadness
but she
is still with me. . . .

BALLADE OF SUMMER SADNESS

>—For Fr. David Subu, whose homily
>inspired it

When I was young, each Summer meant a thrill
    Of sheer anticipation—mountain climb,
Or motor boat out on the blue and chill
    Waters of Lake Dunmore! In my prime,
    And hating school!—I wish I had a dime
For every thought I had of playing ball
    Up in Vermont's invigorating clime!
But now the Summer is the worst of all,

The worst of all the seasons. "What? You're ill!"
    Perhaps, but if I were a brilliant mime
I could enact for you how with a will
    Tremendous I discuss for the first time
    With students whom I love the gift sublime
Of true poetic beauty: in the Fall
    And in the Winter, Spring, but—what a crime!
Not in Summer! Summer's worst of all.

What can I do? I'll love to lecture 'til
    I'm dead and gone! Like frankincense or thyme,
It's poetry for me! I'll never shill
    For what is fake, disfigured with dark grime,
    Or rotting in a pit of stinking lime. . .
I worship at Calliope's high hall!

But—class once over, I can't hear her chime:
For me the Summer is the worst of all.

L'envoi

O, Father David! "*Isn't it a* shime?"
(Or shame, excuse me) that this does befall
　　Myself, a sinner? ("Shime" was my last *rhyme*...)
For me the Summer is the worst of all.

MALMESBURY

Vivekananda spoke of spiritual East and material West;
I wonder if he ever had a chance to view the best
Norman sculpture England boasts, apostles twelve in two
Tympana of golden stone, with angels flying through.

As the angels pass ahead, they sweep with scripture's Word
The heads of these disciples, touched by each celestial bird;
See them raise their hands, and twist their heads astonished by
The sudden stroke as spirit does their hearts electrify.

Beneath their feet, the saw-tooth arches hearken back in time
To Anglo-Saxon days, when Christian roots were in their prime.
Just now the lightning bolt descends and charges drapery folds
With sharpened lines of synaesthesia: ecstasy in golds!

Oh Swami! Take another look. Material veneer
Will melt before your gaze, revealing underneath a sheer
Spiritual charisma that we share with you, though we
Forget it, sadly, and without it fade all tragically.

BEA, ABBEY, GARDEN

Bea, how can you know? And yet you know,
Echoing mottled pink upon your cap
Behind there's mottled stone from long ago
Carved into magic figurings; mayhap

You've seen it on the abbey entrance, though
It seemed to crumble as you looked: the Christ
So delicately crucified! Below,
His legs athwart pierced through the frame incised

To contain who will not be contained:
He contains all else, that is, His Love
So hard to understand is still maintained
In Grandpa's closer smile not far above.

Scholars in the schools have toiled and strained
To link it all, the God, the growing girl
That's you, pretty in pink, the windows stained
With glorious colors, which you see unfurl

Their banners in the garden, soon to fade,
And yet they never fade; while seasons pass
The Abbey there behind you glows like jade
That's stood here for 900 years! Its glass

For Bea, for Grandpa, for the Garden laid
Before Creation, waiting 'till time ends!
Meanwhile, now is always, gentle maid:
We all shall meet as past in present blends.

A PRINT BY BRUEGHEL

St. Jerome is huddled down inside a hidden cave
Barely discernible to a world where mad fanatics rave.
He's chosen a corner where nature's graces and the ploughs of man
Do better work, the work of God, where heroes also ran:

Like Atalanta, Heracles, and those of Jason's crew
Inspired and sometimes victimized by gods the Greeks once knew.
But now Jerome and his tame lion feel a higher calling
Even than theirs, flamed by Love, that burns all that's appalling.

FACE TO FACE

I miss my students! Keeping up the pace
By teaching them on-line now faute de mieux;
But still I miss them, since there is—parbleu!
No substitute for teaching face to face.

I try to show them passion, also grace,
But on a screen—although that be my goal—
There's nothing but an image, there's no soul:
No substitute for teaching face to face.

Technology has put us in a race
To do things faster, easier, but, no,
It's really not a better way to go,
No substitute for teaching face to face.

My love for Shakespeare I can surely trace
To Midwood High School, where a man named Joe
Grebanier simply read him, strong and slow!
Electrifying me, just face to face.

Oh Lord, this virus is a real disgrace,
Infecting, killing, striking people who
Are on their knees and praying that, soon, You
Will let us meet each other face to face.

OÙ EST LA VAILLANCE D'ANTAN?

Où sont les neiges d'antan?
—Villon

How have we lost our courage, O my Muse!
The daily headlines surely must confuse
The reader who's aware of how men acted
In history when not by fear distracted.

Recall how Noah, led by God, set sail,
The last man standing, who knew if he'd fail
The human race would perish, and all creatures,
Unless God re-created their dear features.

Two words he banished from vocabulary:
What if. . .? As Noah undertook his very
Dangerous mission, 'til olive branch and dove
Showed him and his the power of Faith and Love.

Or watch Odysseus departing Troy,
As hostile gods upon his route deploy
Scylla, Charybdis, Polyphemus, and
Circe, who would touch men with her hand

And turn them into beasts, fate worse than death!
The Sirens too, whose songs might cut the breath
Of men intoxicated by their beauty,
Or brought to Lotus Land, stripped of their duty.

Columbus, Muse, bring back, with his ships three
Across the vast Atlantic sailing free
Unfrightened by what on the other shore
He might encounter—full of hope in store.

Again, O Clio! conjure pioneers
Venturing on the plains through months and years
With wives and children, seeking a new world
While savage tribes their war-flags there unfurled.

Shall we go on? Today these men are spurned
By our "historians" who have not learned
The lessons thou dost teach, instead revise
Your annals to denounce all enterprise.

Could we be their mere students? Could we be
Participants in decadence, as we
Confront a new disease in panicked terror?
Are we prudent? Or in tragic error?

Is man a striving Angel, or machine?
An aspirant to Holiness, or mean
In aspiration? From what we have seen
Today he only yearns for quarantine.

FATHER

You were old when I was just a boy—
Now I'm old, and you remain the same:
What I then took for age was really joy—
The sad joy that eschews both wealth and fame.
The eyes I thought were closed were opened wide
To view the inner universe of soul:
Here is a man whose warmth came not from pride,
But from a passion to discern the whole.
Not old, not young, but wise beyond mere time,
Believing only what the eye could see,
And seeing beyond self—the very prime
His only goal... And that included me:
I always knew that as he gazed above
Within his gaze flowed never-doubted love.

FOR SOPHIE LAM

Sophie, a museum may be dark
To hordes of visitors who cannot see—
They think they can, but that erroneously—
But you will bring in light, which those that mark

True beauty will be gladdened by! Your fingers
Have gently woven hairs like silk, as others
In ancient days wove patterns taught by mothers,
Forming a goddess of light whose radiance lingers.

Such elegance and dignity these days
Are rarely met, but in you come together
To show the world what "Lady" means, in ways

The courts of China once displayed—a feather
Of a Bird of Paradise might be your sign
As signature to tapestry-design.

FRANCE OR CHINA IN PROSPECT PARK

The green is thick and dark , as in Courbet;
I wish to enter, there to be alone,
But the picture just affords no way.

"Dark and hidden" as said by Wang Wei,
Where he sat and plucked his lute's soft tone,
The green is thick and dark, as in Courbet.

One friend of his appeared with bright display,
The moon that night, which time to time had shone,
But this picture just affords no way.

Courbet's darkness partly does dismay,
Hiding hope for us of flesh and bone;
Here green is thick and dark, as in Courbet.

Men may brood but they must also play,
They must take such copses as their own,
But the picture just affords no way.

Wang if he were with us just might say
Neither Yin nor Yang we may disown.
The green is thick and dark, as in Courbet,
But the picture just affords no way.

GREY POTOMAC

November 18, 2015

These waterbirds, skimming the Potomac—
Choppy wavelets swaying the fishing dock
I sit on, with my dog—are they the moment?
Or are they memories?—They will be soon,
As everyone must know, but not right now.
The question conjures other city rivers,
The Hudson, maybe, back in old New York:
I'd sit there gazing at the seagulls floating,
Before my lessons in classical guitar.
So similar. The mood is similar too,
Greyness of feeling, as the sky is grey,
The moving clouds, the water—everything.
Those seagulls were the moment, yes, they were
So many moments, but . . . I know I sensed
That they were passing from me even as
I looked at them, and these, they too are passing,
Not only over water, but in time, right now,
Or time is passing, what the poets ever
Have told us of, happening here and now
And always. But then, they're not the moment,
Or—the moment has no substance: once say, "It is,"
And already it is not. And so insist
The Buddhists with the poets. Emptiness
Is ever here before us, yet not here.
How many times has this been realized?

By me, by others? Others yet to come
Will realize it too. And yet Blake says
The poet's work is done between pulsations
Of an artery, that is, *between*
The non-existent moments! How did he
Achieve that realm? And will it ever yawn
For me to enter? If it does, these birds
And New York's seagulls may be there in flight,
Or bobbing on the water, as before—
True Heaven, I would think. So what we see
Around amidst the greyness is a glimpse
Of Heaven, and frustrated visionaries
Have yet to find the way to travel there.

IN MEMORIAM STEVE BERG

September 13, 2021

A knock heard at the gate, so gentle, meek;
Yet the cosmos echoes with the tone,
As ever when each homing sheep, alone,
Approaches finally what all must seek.
Sung low a song arises, soft, not weak,
And angels chant responses round the throne:
Fragrance from Empyrean is blown,
Gate opening, the sheep gets his first peek. . . .

Steve Berg now knows what we may only know
If we like him are granted that the veil
Be lifted on what, promised long ago,
Is fallen world turned paradise. The Grail
Offered to his lips brims with life-blood,
Wine of wines tapped from the holy Rood.

IN MEMORIAM TOM BERTONNEAU

2021

Tom wrote "The Truth is Out There"; face to face
With Uncreated Light among the ranks
Of blessèd ones, he offers now his thanks
To One transfigured, monarch of that place.

Around the Throne great authors, twenty-four,
Join in the adoration, welcome Tom
As he who grasped the spirit-soothing balm
Conveyed through them; the angels bow or soar.

Of course! Tom somehow sensed past all heart-ache
That it would be like this; the veil removed,
He'd see not *with* but *through* his eyes as Blake

Enjoined us all, suffering One who loved
And rose for us to teach us our dependence,
Revealing the humaneness of Transcendence.

LAMENT FOR PRINCE PHILIP

Today I mourn for news just brought to me:
Prince Philip, Duke of Edinburgh, glowing
In angelic light, *Cloud of Unknowing*
The path he's followed our Lord to see.

Not English, I, though it's the language I,
American, was raised in, came to love
For words aspiring towards what is above,
And reaching it, in Wordsworth's poetry,

Or Blake's. And I can say that I have trod
Where Philip did, Mount Athos, sacred soil
To those whose souls are set on finding God.

His love of the Transcendent helped despoil
Battalions of his enemies, mere fools!
His goodness, nay, his greatness transcends rules.

IN THE WAITING ROOM

Jennifer and Sarah, Jane and Sue:
You're lovely all, in white! Enjoy the view,
Enjoy the conversation, and the breeze
That wafts from ocean islands through the trees.

Somewhere in Massachusetts, or in Maine?
Did you arrive by carriage, or by train?
Are you four cousins, sisters, maybe friends?
You stand or sit on one of our land's ends,

Four flowers beautifying barren rock,
And here defying time's inexorable clock.
It seems that Jennifer and Jane discourse
About the latest scandal, or race-horse,

Or maybe something elevated: art?
Or music? Or religion? Or the heart
That one of them has given to a wooer?
Their words were earnest, but they now grow fewer.

Meanwhile, Sue looks on, and tries to follow
The dancing of their thoughts; she will not wallow
Any further into their conversation;
She merely watches Jane's peregrination

From topic on to topic. Sarah, though,
Is interested not at all. Winds blow
Directly through her hair as she alone
Fronts ocean—and well matches ocean's tone:

So far she gazes, at the islands there?
Or further, does she follow ships that glare,
Points of white fire upon the deepest blue?
I cannot tell, and neither, friend, can you.

We cannot question them, they're not in time,
Their moment lifted, caught in paint and rhyme,
And by a hand that even might have touched
The soft white dresses that it has here brushed.

Frank Weston Benson signed and dated it,
1909, which makes a perfect fit
With what they wear; in 1951
The painter died, but these girls had begun

A journey that would lift them from the plane
Of ordinary life, against the grain
Of time's procession season unto season,
As artistry has given us a reason

To ponder this: A brief epiphany,
A moment of the purest harmony
Of self with self or self with ocean, earth,
Or tree or rock gives transience rebirth,

All unanticipated. Someone sees
The lovely ladies, feels the lovely breeze,
And paints them, though themselves they're unaware,
So they now sit or stand forever there.

How real are they? Did they in fact exist
At all? Or was the painter's soul impressed
By images like dreams, or memories
Of other pictures, which by faint degrees

Became a part of his own inner world
Until upon the canvas they unfurled?
Who knows? The painter too might be confused
About the source. Perhaps he too was used

In turn by someone else, one yet above
Himself, and motivated by a love
So great that it would wish to take what passes—
The ocean breezes, and the flowers and grasses,

The pristine dresses, fluttering in air,
The maidens, oh so beautiful! who are there
Just for the afternoon—and to translate
These signs of something more where temporal fate

Can't harvest them for death with his grim scythe!
Where they forever can ascend, not writhe
In agony once moment's glory's gone,
Ascend where all of this we look upon

Becomes a stage for all of us who burn
With longing for pure beauty, we who yearn
To walk forever on the sacred sod
That's being painted for us by our God.

MAN BEFORE A PAINTING

for Robert Harrist
 in memory of what was a brief moment or an eternity
  in the Art Institute of Chicago

A man before a painting: he's alone
As seen by others, not in solitude;
Focus on his eyes, his attitude,
Perceive that from this worldly realm he's gone,

Seeing "through, not with, his eye" as Blake
Knew well. And here before him is a saint
Receiving the stigmata. Does he faint
From excruciating pain? For Christ's sake

He bears and he transcends it, raptly stares
Into the gaze of God as, stunned, he kneels
On Zurbarán's glowing stone—dun, sun-baked;

For the man, as for Francis, thirst is slaked
By Beauty, Truth and Goodness that he feels
Before—a painting? no, before the Stars.

IN WESTERN TURKEY

Ayvali, Anatolia: 1922,
Year of suffering
Bewailed in song....
—1986. Two tourists,
pilgrims rather, one myself,
the other Anna, beloved
wife, walking; hilly streets
beneath balconies
that overhang. A boy,
10 years old? steps out
as if from nowhere, points
and walks, we follow him
through narrow winding streets,
until a square unfolds, a church,
Orthodox, abandoned.
He leads us in,
All barren, no furniture,
iconostasis gone, but walls
show pale bluish icons worn away,
once beautiful, yet now
chill, haunting in their
martyrdom, their *eyes*,
each one of them, scratched out.
We stare, silent. Shocked.
The boy looks on.
Outside,
the protecting veil of
Mediterranean skies.

JUST ONE LEAF

A single leaf
Contains enough
To point us to
The end of grief.

But only the Wise
Can read this map,
While others are limited
To their eyes.

All we need
To know is here,
If only we
Can wisely read.

The color, green,
Alone contains
All colors that
Around are seen.

The verso hides
The recto, though
Just turn it over—
There are two sides.

The other one
Though hidden now
May be discerned
Beneath the sun.

This is all,
A microcosm
Vast, expansive,
Though so small.

"To see the world
In a grain of sand"
As Blake says well,
Herein unfurled.

THE PARADOX

—a sonnet for Nick and Emilia

Lydia Rose and Lucy Hyacinth,
Two girls like flowers newly have been born,
Each worthy of a statue on a plinth,
Or will be when their goddess-selves see morn.

But now their parents' happiness transcends
All worldly chatter, so embracing flesh
And rejecting it—these clashing trends—
Are really one, as soul and body mesh.

Thus proclaim Zen-Masters, though until
The Hand divine has lifted us above,
We cannot see the union; Satan's mill

Grinds cruelly, but Joy announces Love,
And Rose and Hyacinth, the precious twins
Prove both ways evil withers, goodness wins.

MUNDAKA UPANISHAD

Two birds in a tree
And both of them me!
The first eats the fruit;
The other rests mute.
The first I mistake
For myself awake.
The other can see
That *he's* the real me.

ODE TO AN ARTICHOKE

—for Zina

Your name, exotic! Flesh come from the gods!
Straight imbibed, or mixed with cheese or sauce.
The humble plow that down the furrow plods
Leads to a jewel, a ball that Jove might toss.
Olive-green, picked out in muted silver,
Thistle-blossom burgeoning in peace;
For mystery I have been long a delver,
And I remember finding it in Greece,
Deep in your caverns! Yes, we plucked each leaf
And dipped it in the herbal, liquid butter—
Labored surely, to the point of grief—
Yet what we tasted set our hearts aflutter.

Bitter and the sweet, the soft and firm—
Opposites in microcosmic whole—
And as the leaves grew fewer, there, the Germ
Of Being showed itself, the light-green bole
Hidden down so far, down underneath
The leaves now all discarded; the supreme
Ambrosia of the artichoke—the breath
Of life once death has proved the merest dream.

ORIENTATION FOR STUDENTS GOING TO CHINA

A duet by the Director of Fellowships and Graduate Student Support and the Director of the Office for Study Abroad, with chorus of students

"OK. Here goes. You're leaving soon for China!
The PRC! But please leave home your mynah
As birds are not allowed: the avian flu
Might enter China right along with you."

"We wouldn't dream of bringing in the flu."

"But wait a minute. There's a new disease
That might LEAVE China with you, if you please!
It might attack in restaurants, in bars
Or anywhere at all: its name is SARS."

"Alas! Alack! We spend our lives in bars."

"'Severe, Acute'"—how serious that sounds!
"'Res-pir-a-to-ry Syndrome.'" Egad! Zounds!
To make sure you do not come down with it
Please wear these masks wherever you may sit—"

"Well maybe we'll just stand and never sit!"

"—Or stand or walk or lie down! Never take them
From off your face, and do not try to fake them!
The only masks allowed are made in Cuba
By prisoners whose jailer plays the tuba"

("But we thought that they had no jails in Cuba!")

"As hours a day they slave away and sew
These Red Star Brand hygienic, smooth air flow-
Facilitating masks of purest gauze!
(The tuba plays a death-march without pause.)"

"We wouldn't dream of breaking Chinese laws."

"Let's see. What else. Oh yes! Please ride a bike
Instead of bringing driver's license. Hike
Or simply walk if you hate bikes: NO CARS
ALLOWED. And once again, look out for SARS."

"Oh no! We cannot live without our cars."

"Look out for it in classrooms, hotel rooms,
In student hostels, everywhere, bring brooms
To sweep the ground before you! Even Mars
Is now infected with the germs of SARS."

"And our next destination will be Mars!"

"And when you're back, you will be quarantined
For forty days and nights, and also screened
With CATSCANS, MRI'S out the whazoo:
We must be sure that SARS is not in you."

"We promise solemnly that our whazoos
Will be quite free of SARS and also booze."

"OUR GOAL SHOULD BE A PLANET WITH FEWER HUMANS"

—Washington Post Opinion, June 12, 2024

Let's assume the writer is correct:
The challenge now is for us to detect
The best techniques for lowering population,
Increasing deaths, decreasing copulation.

Or maybe Law would help—*mandate* abortion
For every pregnancy out of proportion,
Like China's quondam "One-Child" policy,
Improving global life for every tree.

But—I am human, could be too humane;
Let's apply AI's robotic brain!
Abortion is too little and too late
For Mother Earth to conquer dire fate.

AI proclaims: choose every other town
And drop upon it bombs all raining down.
Your humans would be decimated, good!
Protecting every wet-land and each wood.

Or better yet: lace every market's food
With cyanide; AI can feel no mood
Such as compassion, or nostalgia, so
This is a quicker way....but *still* too slow!

"I've got it!" chirps AI, "sink dynamite
Into earth's molten center to ignite
A grand explosion thus eradicating
All humans with their trash and defecating."

THROUGH GREEN MIST

Paddling slowly through green mist
The duck is lonely. No Mandarin lover
Is by his side, nor does she hover
Where trees by azure sky are kissed.

This is Prospect Park—but who
Would think this scene serene and pretty
Could thus unfold within a city?
And yet it's there, and yet it's true.

When I was four or five I played
Along these shores, among these trees
In Summer's heat and Winter's freeze...
Then we moved. Some memories fade

While some, surprisingly recalled,
As this one is, bear special weight
And seem an icon of one's fate:
Then and now, all free, unwalled.

IMAGE OF AN IMAGE

Shadow of a fence upon a tree,
Wavering black lines on sunset hues;
Fences fence you in or fence you out,
Fences' shadows make it hard to choose.

Trees fenced in, protected from intruder,
Or are they prevented from uprooting,
Flying dragon-like away from cruder
Turmoil to a place where stars are shooting

From nowhere down to Eden, *Hortus conclusus*?
Perhaps these all are shadows on the wall
Of Plato's cave. Mere phantasies confuse us,
But also fascinate. . . . Well, all in all

God only knows. But we enjoy the play
Of Substance, Shadow, inside and without:
And so we will until the final say
Which shall disburden us of our doubt.

SONNET FOR A WRONGED MAN

> —*"The flame of anger consumes itself only."*
> Zeami (Japanese playwright, 1363–1443)
> Translation by Arthur Waley

Dear friend,
... And such it's ever been, since Eve
And Adam brought us to it. Ah, the gall
Of serpents ever in the grass. Now Paul
Is stung as well. One hardly can believe

A man who's striven so hard to retrieve
The Grand Tradition might become a ball
Upon a billiards table. Yet the Fall
Has left no one exempt from Satan's sieve.

But like the grain, just leave behind the chaff,
And keep the part that nurtures; as new crop,
You'll grow and flourish and then with a laugh

Dismiss your anger, whose flame without stop
"Destroys itself alone," Zeami tells us,
And is the only enemy that fells us.

SONNET TO ALEXANDRIA

in the manner of Longfellow

Venice floats on water, or it hovers;
Paris fronts the Seine, the ancient Thames
Is London's berth: and each one of these gems
A yearned-for destination for all lovers.

Alexandria! Potomac flows
Where you have thriven since our nation started!
And even when the South and North had parted,
You were the crossroads of our mutual woes.

You the heart, Potomac then the vein
Conveying lifeblood to and from the sea;
Now you are a link in the vast chain

That joins the past and present, seamlessly.
Though smaller than the others, noble fate
Inscribes in history that you are great.

STARS AND SOUL

A sonnet for Professor Jonathan Lunine,
astronomer *extraordinaire*

Once again, the morning news, despair
At sensing just how distantly we've strayed:
Every morning hopelessly I've prayed
That someone might emerge to clear the air

Of Academe from mere emotion, care
For Truth, and like old knights, come to the aid
Of two maids—Science, Religion—wrongly splayed
Apart, yet quondam partners, lovely pair.

Professor Lunine! You now throw a light
Where darkness dominated, mind incisive
To penetrate the anger-driven blight

Of mere hostility, to be decisive
In finding Truth wherever it may lurk:
Knight in armor, doer of God's work.

TO STEVE ADDISS

Looking out from beneath the bamboo,
What do you see? Is there anything
You don't see? And what do you sweep
With your broom? I cannot answer.
You too may have no answer.

But you have seeking, you have love
For what you see, and want to sweep it
Into powerful strokes and tender,
Bamboo leaves or knots,
These movements of your heart.

This I can say: I have felt these movements
And as leaf to branch, knot
To knot, fresh and cool,
They have intertwined with my heart,
That's why you are my friend.

Do you see friends from under the bamboo?
"Corporeal friends," says Blake,
"Are spiritual enemies." Would Sengai
Say the same? You have been
These years, my spiritual friend.

Keep sweeping, playing, potting,
Writing, all of this your breathing,
Praying, may the prayer be heard.
I have heard it. The cosmos
Has heard it. It is heard.

IN MEMORIAM STEPHEN ADDISS

April 12, 2022

A scholar, staff in hand, is climbing
          up the mountainside;
He stops and gazes at a waterfall,
          and hears it singing,
Hears embedded in this sound
          a temple bell, low ringing,
His goal when at the summit,
          which he'll reach without a guide.

Steve! I've climbed along with you!
          Now I grieve, as tide
And time have parted us,
          and I am sorrowfully clinging
To precious memories alone,
          but they at least are bringing
Some comfort to a soul bereaved,
          as memories will abide.

But no, there's more: your spirit
          hovers still in bowls you molded,
In books you wrote, in words you said,
          in the mirror of the heart:
There your eyes still scintillate,
          there your love's enfolded:

"The ruins of Time build Mansions
              in Eternity," Blake's dart
Of fire penetrates life and death—
              together with him we
Will humbly pray to meet again,
              friends in Eternity.

COOLING RAIN: TIME TRICKED?

After passing comes a cooling rain—
Sent through mail by one thought long passed on.
On the porch, I gazed at it: upon
The wrapping in his writing—am I sane?—

My name and address, freshly written, black
With Chinese ink he used for all his writing,
And his home-return address, inciting
Great wonderment which took me all aback.

Thick wrapping slowly layer by layer removed,
A Japanese box of wood appeared, well-brushed
In Japanese—his well-known writing. Hushed,
I deciphered: *Bamboo Sound*—well-loved

Signature, and title: *Cooling Rain*;
Verso of the cover, Englished, same
And cinnabar seals of his. This was no game,
But real work by ADDISS, as was plain.

Then, opened and revealed, scintillating
With subtle greens and blues and greys slow-flowing
As flow the clouds and all the cosmos, glowing,
Microcosm with energy pulsating,

A bowl for tea in ceremony served,
Or just for viewing, meditating, Zen.
I kissed it, put it on a shelf, and then
Let love flow freely, albeit unnerved.

DAUGHTER IN SEARCH OF. . . .

Named for *haiku* poet by her father,
Heart left yearning by love unresolved—
Something like a riddle yet unsolved—
Redbud blossoms, though, for her to gather

Every year to represent a heart
Never fully seen or fully heard
In a world that's void or, no, absurd. . . .
Still she senses that these are a start.

Yes, she's destined to be touched or kissed
By what isn't empty and has meaning,
Though below it might seem somehow missed,

Descending to her in form of a dove,
Unexpected! She will then be gleaning
From this miracle full father's love.

TANUKI

March 14, 1980, recording a dream

Clay tanuki in author's collection

The ocean leaves a body on the shore,
strange corpse, silvery fur
with spots of pinkish red. . .
This is no fish, a mammal
we pull up on the beach
and save in the fork of a tree.
And then—*how lovable!*—strange rebirth!
The silvery grooves of his coat
begin to give off light,
he sits upright,
leans back against the trunk,
and pulls out—a pipe! which he
begins to smoke. White clay bowl
in hand, he looks both left and right,

lounging there, viewing the scene
with wit and warmth. Tanuki!
Have you returned,
how lovable!—to guide us
toward new light?

THE ABSCONDING OF JOEL

And as horsemen, so shall they run—thus writeth Prophet Joel!
Could that be why our Joel, the dog, abominates control?
Eight times already—yea, twice four!—our dog hath run away,
Houdini in his heyday never could escape this way!

Each weakness in the backyard fence, each loosened gate, each hole
Discovered quite immediately our latest doggie, Joel:
One day while two fence-fixers were a-working on the fence,
Right under their poor noses Joel escaped and fled from hence!

But yesterday was worst of all! Our Joel, so very fleet,
Was tracked by his new GPS unto North Chambliss Street—
Or rather to the thickest woods that line that distant route—
And so I jumped into our car and drove in hot pursuit!

All dark it was when I got there, deserted was the road,
Until a man appeared and said, "Behind yon brick abode
I saw him run!" I dashed into the woods, but my cell phone
Fell from my clutching hand when I heard distantly the tone

Of doggie howl! The home computer now could not tell me
Whereunto Joel had wandered! I ran headlong on a tree,
And then was held a prisoner by clinging, ropey vines
Which almost seemed like monsters with nefarious designs.

And then—a flash! A doggie-shape like Joel's went dashing by
Beyond the thicket! On his collar, blue light like an eye
Was winking at me! Yes, his GPS was flashing now
That he was far from home! "I'm here!" I shouted, "*JOEL*...." But how

Could that succeed? Joel is a hound, and when he's on the scent
He does not heed my voice at all, instead he is hell-bent
On tracking down the fox, the deer, the squirrel—*bloody hell!*
Exhausted, as Joel disappeared back into that dark dell

I realized that I had failed! returned to my old car,
And drove back home, defeated, sad, and wished home were a bar.
I went to bed; I tried to sleep; then, hours later, "JOEL!"
My wife cried out delighted: he was back! God bless his soul!

THE HISTORY OF FOUR BLIPS

My barber stopped his clip:
My nose lay in my lap!
"Oh no!" He screamed, "Oh crap!"
"It's just a minor blip!"

My pants gave out a rip,
My right leg to expose:
My class woke from its doze:
"It's just a minor blip!"

A snap in my left hip
Made walking quite a pain;
The pain shot through my brain.
"It's just a minor blip!"

The Last Trump blared, "PIP PIP!"
The dead from graves emerged!
The cosmos sideways verged:
"Now, *that's* a major blip!"

THE ONLY ANTIDOTE

    after reading Freeman Wills Crofts,
    Antidote to Venom (1939)

George was manager of a great Zoo,
Famous for its vipers and its snakes.
He was good at everything to do
With animals and worked hard for their sakes.

But back at home, his life was lonely, tense;
Though married, love—if ever it existed—
Had vanished from both hearts. An iron fence
Kept them apart, and only chill persisted.

And there were money problems; bills were paid,
But barely, and some debt accumulating;
A rich aunt on the brink of death might fade
At any moment, so, anticipating

Her demise George kept a dim flame burning
Of forlorn hope. Meanwhile, an old professor
Of Herpetology aimed at discerning
How viper venom carefully in lesser

Doses might cure cancer! George was proud
To let him use the Snake House for his work.
But failing health his future might becloud,
And then, his lawyer-nephew (what a jerk!),

Himself was *eager* for his uncle's death,
The gentleman being even wealthier
Than George's aunt. One day, the uncle's breath
Just stopped. . . . Before, the nephew, stealthier

Than is entirely admirable, had gambled
All his money down the drain, so he
Embezzled funds from his own clients, rambled
Back to the casino shamelessly,

And lost their funds as well, these now including
George's legacy, which he controlled!
When he told George, our hero's throat occluding,
The lawyer took a measure brash and bold.

Holding George by pistol, he proposed
A partnership between them to dispatch
The old professor (uncle). He supposed
That George as serpent-expert just might catch

And milk for venom a deadly Raffles viper;
He—the nephew—might arrange what would
Appear to all an accident: a sniper,
Using the venom, he'd put paid for good

To his own uncle. Legacy in hand,
The nephew would repay to George the sum
He had embezzled—more, in fact. How grand!
At first George hesitated but, by gum,

He finally agreed. And rather soon
The plot was laid and executed well.
The Inquest found "death by an accident;"
And all they had to do was wait. But Hell

Opened wide its jaws, and sucked George in!
A man of no religion, he had thought
That "conscience" was a myth, and also "sin,"
But Oh! he suffered for what he had wrought,

Raskolnikov *redux*. Now suicide
Came to his mind, the first time in his life,
And so to suffocate by gas he tried,
But no, he was in grip of spiritual strife,

And knew he must confess before he could!
About this time, police and Scotland Yard
Brought in the nephew, and they understood
There must be an accomplice, but so hard

It was to finger anyone. Just then
Our George walked in, surrendered, and confessed.
Soon found guilty, sitting in the pen,
Awaiting execution, he felt—*blessed!*

He felt cleansed and calm! And without fear
Awaited gallows-hanging! Was this odd?
Or was it that this man had felt the mere
Peace of knowing he'd been cleansed by God?

THE PHYSICIST AND THE BEE—A DIALOGUE

A physicist said to a bee:
"You *cannot* fly! I cannot see
How built the way you are, my friend,
Your take-offs don't abruptly end!"

The bee said to the physicist:
"You *cannot* think! Though you insist
Your brain cells can, to speculate
Suggests a power far too great!

"You think *about* your thought, professor,
Implying you're the proud possessor
Of something immaterial,
The thing, dear sir, once called the soul.

"So both of us transcend in ways
Quite unsuspected in these days:
Just one thing waits to be confessed—
We both of us by God are blessed!"

THIRD PARTY HARASSMENT

If you overhear
Two people conversing
And something traversing
The thin atmosphere

Offends you profoundly,
Brings tears to your eyes,
It would be most wise
To denounce them roundly.

Invoke Title IX
And report the talk;
Don't wimp out and balk
At drawing the line.

Think third party smoke:
Man smokes a cigar—
Although he is far
From you—not a joke!—

A second breathes in
The foul, evil fumes,
Then walks several rooms
To yours. First man's sin

Now tickles your nose!
Alas! cancer hovers
For you and your lovers
(That's fourth hand, God knows!)

This must be reported!
Our campus, smoke-free,
Bans smoking for me
And for them! Someone snorted!

Offended, I faint!
My head hits the floor,
Concussion and more. . . .
Yes, to be a Saint

In our secular realm
Means telling all this
To the feminist Miss
Who is now at the helm.

Examples galore
Will come to you. Tip
Of the iceberg, your trip
Leads you through Hades' door.

THOUGHTS ON A PHOTO OF KAI

KAI looks out; his eyes see everything
With wonder; as if we would always sing
Instead of talk. But we have lost what he
Does every instant, purely, naturally.

William Blake urged us to see not *with*
Our eyes but *through* them to the very pith
Of what is there, the *inscape* (Hopkins) Kai
Is astonished every instant by.

For him the veil is always lifted, so
He views the spirit hovering high and low,
In sky, on ground, in every tree above,
His vision flashing with his parents' love

Towards this the world, alas! now veiled for us,
As we have parted from it; too much fuss
Obscures the field, dims the clarity
That gives to him its power, incessantly.

THOUGHTS ON THE "CUCUMBER-SHAPED" OBJECT FROM OUTER SPACE

According to the newspapers,
        an object quite bizarre
Is rushing through our solar system,
        having come from far,
And Harvard Chairman of Astronomy,
        one Avi Loeb,
Says he thinks it just might be
        an alien-made probe!

Others, soberer than Avi,
        rising from their slumber,
Immediately exclamed in awe,
        "It looks like a cucumber!"
Woody Allen, you'll recall, oh reader!
        made a movie,
Sleeper, back in '73, about a very groovy
Future in which giant veggies, as well as giant fruits
Are engineered genetically—*cucumbers* also, toots!

(But wait a sec, old H.G. Wells way back in zero-four
Put out his book, *Food of the Gods*, with giant fruits and more.)

Anyway, the thing-a-ma-bob, for those remaining sane,
Is almost certainly a rock, no product of a brain.
And we must ask ourselves, again,
                why have our "smartest" men
Lost their wits entirely, and will do so again?

The answer, sir, is *Flucht vor Gott* as Max Picard knew well,
The "Flight from God," involving every in-tell-ec-tu-al.

And without God there's left—the Void, something Nature hates,
(*Horror vacui*) and therefore fills
                with crazy op-i-ates.

And that includes those "aliens" way up in outer space,
Designing probes to search our world
                as they our tech outpace.
We used to call them angels, or *apsaras*, or—oh, well,
You get the notion. Without spirit, Void is left—or Hell.

UNMASKING

> —*O the mind, mind has mountains, cliffs of fall. . . .*
> Gerard Manley Hopkins

We've layers within us, each will ever ask,
"Which is the real me?" Or "Can I make
Myself just as I wish, may I just take
My appetites, carve each as a mask,

Then wear it sometimes?" Undertake this task
If you work not for *truth*, but for the sake
Of total self-invention, thus partake
Of spirits brewed in Fantasy's own cask.

But "What is truth?" asked Pilate, we recall,
And now again philosophers reprise
His question in their rhetoric, a fall

From pilgrimage to merest wandering,
Forgetting that beneath all masks there lies
An Icon of the Highest, foundering.

THE DEAN ADDRESSES THE FACULTY

"Dear colleagues, I announce a full-court press
To catch up with the other institutions
Already making major contributions
To education: we must now *assess*!

"All other schools are doing it: the stress
Of influence compels us to as well.
To do things differently would be pure hell!
And that is why we simply must *assess*.

"To keep up with the ivies, thus to bless
Our reputations for accreditation,
We simply *must* begin our own migration
Away from 'test' or 'grade' and towards *assess*.

"The difference may seem subtle but—confess
That testing, grading, can no longer be
Appropriate for the Twenty-First Century:
All else is new, and so we shall *assess*.

"And how? Aha! The folks out at Loch Ness
For centuries were brainwashed by tradition
Intoxicating them with superstition.
But now the sociologists *assess*:

"'Of all reports of sightings of this "Nessie,"
We find that 91.9%
Are utterly unworthy of consent.
The rest are even worse.' Ah, how *assessy*

"Those scientists! Inspiring!—I digress.
Now, back to us. If you are not inspired,
If you are too old-fashioned, if you're wired
To do the same old thing, I now *assess*

"That you must be coerced. OK, unless
You now *assess* your students, you will be
Demoted, and then charged a special fee:
$550 each semes-

"Ter 'til you conclude, or 'til you guess
That you must join the bandwagon, parade
Along with us until our school is made
A model laboratory of. . . *assess*—

"*Ment*. I think it must be quite unnec-
Essary to say anything beyond
What I have indicated here. I'm fond
Of brevity. Goodbye. And now—*assess*."

WELCOME TO THE INSTITUTE

There was now at last a real chance for fallen Man to shake off that limitation of his powers which mercy had imposed upon him as a protection from the full results of his fall.
—C.S. Lewis, *That Hideous Strength* (1945)

Dear colleagues, your Vice-President
               for Engineering Life
Announces with the greatest pride
               the end of human strife!
I know you really can't believe
               what you believe you're hearing:
But welcome to the Institute
               of Bio-Engineering!

Today we open wide the doors
               of our new Institute,
And history lacks precedent
               for what will be its fruit:
A human being, flawless, so
               remarkably endearing,
That all will love the Institute
               of Bio-Engineering!

A human who will never fight,
        but always live in peace,
A human who will never eat
        a diet cooked in grease,
A human who will never go a-wine-ing
        or a-beering:
The product of our Institute
        of Bio-Engineering!

Each perfect individual
        will be thus engineered:
No rape of gals by guys! Instead
        all humans will be queered
So that in future, men at men
        and gals at gals all leering,
We all will thank the Institute
        of Bio-engineering.

In other words, no children
        will annoy us anymore!
We'll clone all humans ready-made
        then send them out the door
To join the race of perfect persons
        for which we are gearing
Here at our wondrous Institute
        of Bio-Engineering!

No sickness, conflict, crime at all—
    the flaws we all deplore
So elegantly engineered
    that they'll exist no more!
If I could cry, my eyes right now
    with joy would be all tearing,
Except that in the Institute
    of Bio-Engineering

My sadness and my happiness
    were engineered away!
That's right! Myself, I am a clone!
    We all will be some day.
Meanwhile, let me assure you all,
    there's nothing to be fearing:
Just trust all to the Institute
    of Bio-Engineering.

YE EARLIE HISTORIE OF YE TREPANE

In medieval Munich, a man
Thought, "Why not attempt the trepan?"
The reason he hit on this plan
Was strange: Here is how it began. . . .

Herr Eckhart was cousin to one
Whose fame had burst forth like the sun:
Meister Eckhart his name, and a ton
Of light had exploded its gun

In his mind! "Yea, the Castle of God
Is within! We may feel downtrod,
But deity—this may sound odd!—
Is *in* us: pea in a peapod!"

Now our hero, quite on the contrary,
Believed not in God, nor in fairy,
Nor in anything overly airy,
And certainly not Virgin Mary.

But with the new word from his cousin,
His noggin began loudly buzzin'
With thoughts not a few—say a dozen—
More common to priest or muezin.

"I know that I never could buy
That story—just pie in the sky!—
Of some bearded, stern-visaged guy
Up there in the clouds, way too high

"For anyone ever to see him!
Impossible ever to *be* him,
The only thing sensible? Flee him,
If priests simply can't guarantee him.

"But if he's *within*, what a story!
That means that to *me* is the glory!"
And so Eckhart parted locks hoary
To submit to a procedure gory,

A newly invented technique
Called "trepan," because he did seek
The Castle of God! Yes, quite meek,
He only wished to take a peek.

This history now—ah, alas!—
Unto a sad finish must pass:
Poor Eckhart fell, dead, on his ass!
His hemorrhaged blood filled the glass.

CHANSON DE LA NUIT

—in the Manner of Verlaine
for Willow Hai

Now it falls again...
Black pavement glistens; passing lights
Paint the gloom with splashing whites:
Willow in the rain.

Down a hidden lane
Scurrying cat's paws in cold fear
Caught in street light disappear...
Willow in the rain.

Sudden sigh of pain...
Footsteps where a gentleman
Is whispering: "Please, darling Nan!..."
Willow in the rain.

Overhead, a plane,
Softly humming through cloud layers,
Interlude of muffled prayers...
Willow in the rain.

Willow in the rain:
Raindrops weep from branches, bare. . .
Is there anyone to care?

Now alone again.

ORDINATION

for Deacon Kenneth Liu

"The pine trees sing, but not because of wind:"
Thus Han Shan, "Cold Mountain" when translated;
Not many of us ever have been fated
To hear that sacred music. All have sinned

But few turn pilgrim towards the Light God shines,
Light uncreated like the pine trees' song;
The road to Cold Mountain is difficult and long,
But eases when one hears those singing pines.

Kenneth Liu has heard them, and received
Invisible connection past the clouds
To the sacred lineage achieved

When brightest vestments replace mourning shrouds;
He has been shined on by God's holy beacon
And walks the earth ordained as His new Deacon.

   *Han Shan (?early 9th century, Tang Dynasty):

> *Climbing, climbing the road to Cold Mountain,*
> *Road to Cold Mountain that never ends. . . .*
> *The stream flows long, rocks piled everywhere,*
> *The gullies are wide, reeds filling every space.*

The moss turns moist, though untouched by rain,
The pine trees sing, but not because of wind.
Who can overleap the ties of the world
And sit with me among the white clouds?

Translation by Jonathan Chaves

CHRISTMAS

—a sonnet

Each child born relives the blessed day;
Just one is Savior, but each baby glows
With something holy, halo-like, that shows
Participation in a higher way.

Yes, it will be lost; some even say
Recovery from errors and from woes
Inevitable (the onset of the blows
That mean the babe is banished from his play)

Cannot be hoped for. Yet the waning rose
Comes back again next spring in richest shades,
Its seeming death holds promise of rebirth,

And would our Father grace a flower thus,
While leaving us to wallow as life fades?
Or would the way to Heaven be through earth?

PRESANCTIFIED

Is that my friend, woshipping with me?
Is that my priest, imploring our Lord?
Is that my wife? She looks so, but I see
A change transforming her angelically

As she and choir-mates raise all high and free
Musical conveyance of the Word;
All of us together: let's say *we*
Are on the Lent-route to Eternity.

May this river of sound be River of Life,
Let us swim the current fervently
To where there is no doubt, and never strife,

Where we'll be what we were made to be.
When we arrive, O may we truly merit
The smile of Father, Son, and Holy Spirit.

PENTECOST

Apostles seated upstairs, anxiously
Awaiting—something...when in blinding flash
Twelve tongues of fire struck each like a lash
From a cosmic whip of ecstasy:

Their bodies tensed; their souls, electrified,
Were elevated by sheer spiritual lightning
(Know it was *sublime*)—at once both frightening
And transmuting! Twelve voices loudly sighed,

Then changed to speech dictated by the Spirit.
Now outside, assembled from all nations,
Auditors—each one of them could hear it—

Understood in his own language! Stations
Of the Cross had led the world to this:
Commencement of the outflow of true bliss.

www.ingramcontent.com/pod-product-compliance
Lightning Source LLC
Chambersburg PA
CBHW071718040426
42446CB00011B/2114